SCALA

Forest Park Then and Now

Approximately twelve million people use Forest Park each year to visit the region's major cultural institutions—the Saint Louis Zoo, the Saint Louis Art Museum, the Missouri History Museum, the Saint Louis Science Center and The Muny Opera. It also serves as a sports center for golf, tennis, baseball, bicycling, boating, fishing, handball, ice-skating, rollerblading, jogging, rugby, and more. Others come to Forest Park to take advantage of the wide program of special events, or simply to enjoy some respite from urban life.

Below: Children eating ice cream; the ice cream cone was invented in Saint Louis in 1904 at the World's Fair.

Below: "Grand" hardly begins to describe the centerpiece, or the heart of the restoration of Forest Park. The Grand Basin was funded by Emerson and Forest Park Forever.

For more information on Forest Park
http://stlouis.missouri.org/citygov/parks/forestpark/

Forest Park is, however, equally significant from a naturalistic perspective. In a city where 80% of the land has been developed for business, industry, or residential uses, the park serves as a natural oasis; an important source of green space, including some of the oldest forested areas in Saint Louis; a respite for migrating birds; and an integrated ecosystem where humans and nature can interact.

Above: An aerial perspective of the fabulous grounds, fountains, and structures built in the Park for the 1904 World's Fair.

Forest Park is the soul of the city and its survival is essential to the future of the Saint Louis region. In the time since its inauguration, the Master Plan has been completed; there is a new governance and management structure in place; steward-ship and improvements to all the cultural institutions have been introduced; and over 130 million dollars spent in the reconstruction of the Park. As a result, Forest Park has been reinstated to its former glory as the central gathering place of Saint Louis.

Below: The park lands underwent complete reconstruction to prepare for the World's Fair.

Bottom: "Heart of the Park" Schematic Design for Grand Basin and Post Dispatch Lake, as part of the Forest Park Master Plan by H3 Studio.

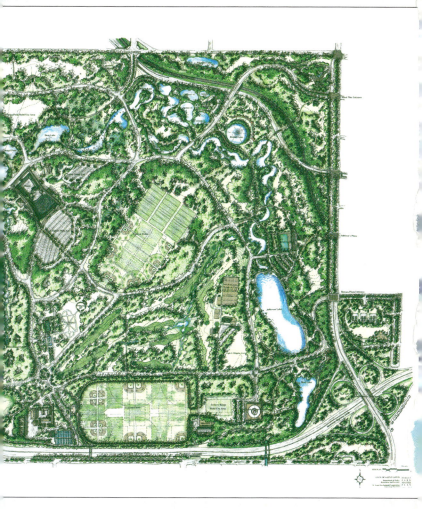

Saint Louis Art Museum

The Saint Louis Art Museum was founded in 1879 as the Saint Louis School and Museum of Fine Arts, an independent entity within Washington University. The Museum was originally located in downtown Saint Louis but relocated to its current home in Forest Park following the 1904 World's Fair. Designed by famed architect Cass Gilbert, the Museum's Beaux-Arts style building bears the inscription "Dedicated to Art and Free to All." The Museum's long-standing commitment to free admission makes it possible for all visitors to have the opportunity to visit the galleries as often as they like throughout the year. Through generations of public support and private benefaction, the Museum has assembled one of the finest art collections in the country.

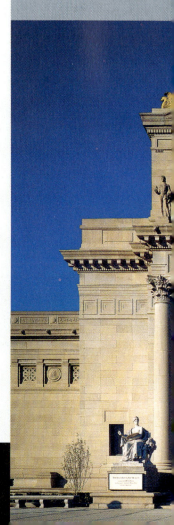

For more information on the Saint Louis Art Museum
www.slam.org
One Fine Arts Dr., Saint Louis, MO 63110-1380
Tel. (314)721-0072

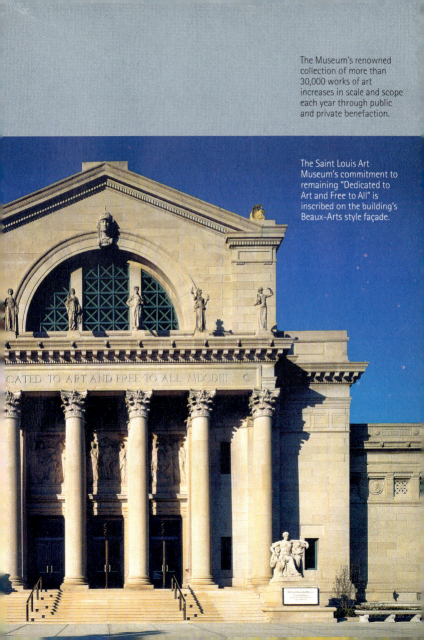

The Museum's renowned collection of more than 30,000 works of art increases in scale and scope each year through public and private benefaction.

The Saint Louis Art Museum's commitment to remaining "Dedicated to Art and Free to All" is inscribed on the building's Beaux-Arts style façade.

Above: The Saint Louis Art Museum has been in Forest Park since 1906, moving from its location in downtown Saint Louis following the 1904 Louisiana Purchase Centennial Exposition.

Below: Designed by architect Cass Gilbert as the Palace of Fine Arts for the 1904 World's Fair, the Museum's dramatic Sculpture Hall was modeled after the Roman Baths of Caracalla.

The Saint Louis Art Museum is one of the nation's leading comprehensive art museums, with collections that include over 30,000 works of art of exceptional quality, from virtually every culture and time period. Areas of notable depth include Oceanic art; pre-Columbian art; ancient Chinese bronzes; American and European art of the late nineteenth and twentieth centuries, with a particular strength in twentieth-century German art. The Museum offers a full range of exhibitions and educational programming generated both independently and in collaboration with local, national, and international partners. It also provides such essential resources as a research library, a varied schedule of special events, as well as restaurants and shops.

With a per-capita attendance that is consistently among the highest of the nation's art museums, it is a leader in making its collections and programs available to a broad public audience. This tradition will continue through the Museum's future growth. The Board of Commissioners of the Saint Louis Art Museum has appointed the London-based David Chipperfield Architects and noted landscape designer Michel Desvigne to design the Museum's planned expansion of its historic building in Forest Park. As authorized in the Forest Park Master Plan, the Museum's expansion is intended to meet its current and future space needs. Both the Museum's 2000 Strategic Plan and Long-Term Space Study, completed in 2003 by Cooper, Robertson and Partners, call for an expansion to accommodate the Museum's growing art collection and improve public amenities.

1: *Bearded Bull's Head*, c. 2600–2550 B.C.
Sumerian
2: *Raftsmen Playing Cards*, 1847
George Caleb Bingham
3: *Stairway at Auvers*, 1890
Vincent van Gogh
4: *Dark Abstraction*, 1924
Georgia O'Keeffe
5: *Water Lilies*, c.1916–26
Claude Monet
6: *Judith and Holofernes*, c.1554
Giorgio Vasari
7: *Madame Roulin*, 1888
Paul Gauguin

Left: At Fragile Forest, chimpanzees, orang-utans, and gorillas explore their spacious new outdoor homes.

Right: The Zoo's inspiring new sculpture, *Animals Always*, is a symbol of future wildlife preservation.

Several of the Zoo's notable historic attractions were built during the 1920s and '30s, including the Bird House, Primate and Reptile Houses, and Antelope exhibit. The Charles H. Hoessle Herpetarium is home to one of the largest collections of reptiles and amphibians in North America. Later, Jungle of the Apes and the Donn & Marilyn Lipton Fragile Forest would provide indoor and outdoor habitats for gorillas, orangutans, and chimpanzees. The Living World is an interpretive center that combines 150 species of live animals with interactive exhibits. In 1986 the Zoo established a state-of-the-art Endangered Species Research Center & Veterinary Hospital. The Research Center also houses the AZA Wildlife Contraception Center for North American zoos.

Above: At the Insectarium, visitors meet an amazing array of invertebrates, including beautiful butterflies flitting through a walk-through geodesic dome.

Below: All aboard! The Zooline Railroad offers a 20-minute narrated tour on a 1¹/₂-mile round trip, with stopover privileges at four stations.

One of the first permanent exhibits constructed in 1921 was the open and moated Bear Pits. The Saint Louis Zoo's emphasis on natural and, wherever possible, unbarred visual displays was emulated by other zoos for decades to come. Under the leadership of its first director, George P. Vierheller, which began in 1922, the Saint Louis Zoo continued to grow in animal exhibits, attendance, and national acclaim. Later, in 1962, Vierheller was succeeded by Marlin Perkins, formerly a Saint Louis Zoo curator, who had gained international fame through his *Wild Kingdom* television program. Perkins brought the viewing public a new awareness of wild animals in exotic locales. It was the Zoo's sixth director, Charles H. Hoessle, who brought the Zoo to modern-day standards in terms of wildlife education, animal management, animal health, and research.

The Saint Louis Zoo

The Saint Louis Zoo has educated, entertained, and earned a place in the hearts of Saint Louisans for generations. With the Louisiana Purchase Exposition in 1904, there began a long and slow process to establish a zoological park. Sure enough, locals were so proud of the giant elliptical Bird Cage, which had been constructed by the Smithsonian Institute for the event, that, at the close of the World's Fair, it was purchased as a permanent feature for the park—one which prompted the formation of a Saint Louis Zoological Society in 1910. The City of Saint Louis set aside 77 acres within Forest Park for a zoo and named a Zoological Board of Control in 1913. State legislation provided that "the zoo shall be forever free," which has kept it accessible to millions of visitors ever since.

Above: About three million visitors come to the Saint Louis Zoo each year, whether for a family outing or a special event.

Right: One of the world's finest zoos, the Saint Louis Zoo is home to 22,300 exotic animals, many of them rare and endangered.

Below: For the centennial of the 1904 Flight Cage, the Zoo transformed the interior into a dramatic cypress swamp with herons, egrets, ibis, and more.

For more information on the Saint Louis Zoo
www.stlzoo.org
1 Government Dr., Saint Louis, MO 63110
Tel. (314) 781–0900

The Saint Louis Zoo strives to save the Grevy's zebra, Amur tiger, and other endangered animals at home and around the world.

Amongst the shops, restaurants, and rides, contemporary attractions began to add some remarkable new dimensions. At the Emerson Children's Zoo, for example, there are friendly animals to see and touch, an assortment of animal shows and programs, educational play activities, and fun for the whole family. The Monsanto Insectarium introduces visitors to the vast world of invertebrates and, at the Saint Louis Zoo's new multi-species spectacle, River's Edge, visitors can follow a path along a mythical river that touches a variety of habitats in South America, Africa, Asia, and North America. At the Zoo's Penguin & Puffin Coast visitors can enjoy the first walk-through habitat of its kind. The Saint Louis Zoo has been named "America's #1 Zoo" by Zagat Survey.

It is no longer enough for zoos to exhibit animals. Today's modern zoo has the much more serious responsibility of educating the public about the need to save the animals in their care as well as those that are still in the wild. The Saint Louis Zoo is among the leaders of international conservation programs. Dr. Jeffrey P. Bonner, President of the Saint Louis Zoo since 2002, initiated the launch of the WildCare Institute, through which the Zoo manages twelve conservation centers around the globe to help endangered species and troubled ecosystems.

Left: Visitors are nose to beak with king penguins, rockhoppers, and gentoos in a unique walk-through habitat at Penguin & Puffin Coast.

In 1927 the Missouri History Museum received national attention when famed aviator Charles A. Lindbergh, who had just completed the first solo transatlantic flight, agreed to lend his trophies, medals, and gifts to the institution for a ten-day period. The Missouri History Museum exhibited the trophies and memorabilia on top of the archaeological cases in an attempt to put the items on display as quickly as possible. The exhibition opened on 25 June 1927, and a local newspaper estimated that 116,000 people viewed the Lindbergh items in the first four days of the exhibition alone. The exhibition's popularity led Lindbergh to agree to extend the loan of the collection; five years later, Lindbergh and his wife, Anne Morrow Lindbergh, donated the extensive collection to the Missouri History Museum.

Today, the Missouri Historical Society calls the Missouri History Museum in Forest Park home. The Museum includes the Jefferson Memorial Building, the first national monument to Thomas Jefferson, which was built with the proceeds from the 1904 World's Fair. Constructed at the official entrance of Forest Park, the building commemorated Thomas Jefferson's role in the Louisiana Purchase. In 1913, thousands of Saint Louisans stood within the building's loggia and on its lawn to watch as Karl Bitter's marble statue of the United States' third president was unveiled. Soon after, the Missouri Historical Society moved into this graceful Beaux-Arts structure, and it became a public museum. Architectural features of the Jefferson Memorial's loggia include six Tiffany pendant light fixtures; ornate Tiffany bronze doors commemorating the Louisiana Purchase Exposition; a rotunda with a beautiful glazed terra-cotta ceiling, designed with a decorative urn motif and the State Seal of Missouri.

The latest addition to the Missouri History Museum is the Emerson Center, which opened in February 2000. Within the Emerson Center's grand hall, many symbols of the Saint Louis region welcome visitors, including a marble and stone floor representing the rivers that invigorate our community, and a sister plane of Lindbergh's famous *Spirit of St. Louis* airplane, built by the same company that produced the original aircraft, is suspended from the 45-foot high ceiling.

The Missouri History Museum

The Missouri Historical Society dates back to 11 August 1866, when forty-seven founding members met in the Old Courthouse and organized the society "for the purpose of saving from oblivion the early history of the city and state." It is best described by its mission statement:

The Missouri Historical Society seeks to deepen the understanding of past choices, present circumstances, and future possibilities; strengthen the bonds of community; and facilitate solutions to common problems.

For more information on the Missouri History Museum
www.mohistory.org
5700 Lindell Blvd, Saint Louis, 63112
Tel. (314)746-4599

Suspended above the
Missouri History Museum's
Grand Hall is a sister-plane
of Lindbergh's *Spirit of
St. Louis* airplane, built
by the same company
that produced the original
aircraft.

Above left: The Missouri History Museum sits at what was the official entrance to the 1904 World's Fair.

Above top and bottom: Karl Bitter's nine-foot statue of Thomas Jefferson sits underneath a richly decorated terra-cotta ceiling.

Left: Commissioned in 1997, the museum's river mosaic represents the powerful role the Mississippi and Missouri Rivers had in shaping Saint Louis' history.

Above: A perennial favorite at The Muny, *Meet Me in St. Louis* celebrates the 1904 World's Fair and Saint Louis' gilded age.

Above right: The Pageant and Masque of 1914 was performed on Art Hill, depicting Saint Louis' history. Thus began the tradition of grand theatre in Forest Park.

Above left: In 1917, The Muny facility began to take a more solid form. Concrete was laid in the auditorium, and a more permanent stage was constructed.

Below left: The Museum's extensive collections consist of over 175,000 artefacts, including treasures related to Lewis and Clark, Charles Lindbergh, the history of aviation in Saint Louis, and much more.

Above: The Emerson Center expansion in 2000 quadrupled the Museum's gallery space. The expansion also features Meriwether's, an award-winning restaurant, and the Louisiana Purchase, the museum shop.

Today, the Missouri History Museum endorses its mission statement through ongoing research, collecting and conservation, exhibitions, educational programming, publications, and community outreach. *Lewis & Clark: The National Bicentennial Exhibition*—a national exhibition that originated at the Missouri History Museum in 2004 and toured the country between 2004 and 2006—features, for example, hundreds of artifacts relating to the Lewis and Clark Expedition that have not been seen together in one place since Meriwether Lewis and William Clark returned to Saint Louis in 1806. The core of the exhibition is formed by materials entrusted to the Missouri History Museum by the Clark and Lewis families.

Above left: Children are welcome at The Muny, both in the audience and on stage. These children from an early Muny production look particularly solemn.

Above right: The *Radio City Rockettes Muny Spectacular* played in 1998. The Missouri Rockets, the original Rockettes, began in Saint Louis.

Below: Since 1919, The Muny has been lighting the summer skies and filling the hills of Forest Park with the sound of music.

The Muny

Few Saint Louisans can remember Forest
Park before The Muny. Since 1919, the
"granddaddy of summer stock theatres"
has created the glamour and grandeur
of live musical theatre on its mammoth
stage. The Muny is a beloved Saint Louis
tradition—a vital and living institution
that flourishes nowhere else on such
a grand scale.

Ten years after the last note from the
World's Fair had faded into memory, Saint
Louis faced another important occasion—
the 150th anniversary of the founding
of the City. To commemorate this event,
a group of civic leaders arranged an
impressive musical history of the city and,
in May of 1914, the Saint Louis Pageant
and Masque was produced on Art Hill in
front of the Saint Louis Art Museum.
Running for a total of four nights, the
7,500-person cast drew a total audience
of about 400,000 people.

For more information on The Muny
www.muny.org
The Muny, Forest Park, Saint Louis, MO 63112
Tel. (314) 361-1900

e success of the performance inspired the
ty fathers to seek other occasions for
and-scale entertainment, and opportunity
me in 1916, the 300th anniversary of the
eath of Shakespeare. Producer and actress
argaret Anglin, parks commissioner Nelson
unliff, and then-mayor Henry Kiel made
walking tour of Forest Park. When they
ached a gently sloping hillside facing a
vel, tree-lined surface, they knew that
ey need look no further. History of a sort
as made that day, because this natural
mphitheatre was to become the scene
today's Muny.

veral Saint Louis traditions were formed
those first long-ago productions. First,
ughly 250 local actors rounded out Miss
nglin's cast of New York artists. Muny
sts still employ many professional local
rformers in chorus and supporting roles,

with lead roles handled by Broadway actors.
A second tradition in the making was the
casting of young unknown performers, who
would later go on to greater glory. A third
important element was the inclusion of
children in the show. Young people appeared
as plough-boys, sowers, reapers, milkmaids,
sweep boys, and May-pole dancers. To this
day, children are welcomed at The Muny,
both on stage and in the audience.

The success led prominent Saint Louisans
to convene in early 1919 to discuss possible
future uses of the outdoor amphitheater.
The committee agreed: "Light opera, by all
means... the more elaborate, the better...
Something spectacular... something majestic
and impressive... Lots of scenery... Lots of
movement... Dancing choruses...Song."
Light opera it was.

Peter Pan. Each summer, at least
one show is produced for children.
Many adults can trace their love of
theatre to their first experience at
The Muny.

uring its first four decades, The Muny led e country, and often the world, in the roduction of operettas. During the 1930s, e famed Shubert Brothers produced at e Muny, which led to history-making eatre in Forest Park. In 1930, for instance, e Muny was the first theatre outside of roadway given permission to produce e spectacular *Show Boat*. In the role of ap'n Andy was the irascible W.C. Fields. roughout the decades, many famous ctors have started out at The Muny, cluding Saint Louisans Betty Grable, ene Dunne, Mary Wickes, and Vincent Price. ther future stars who played The Muny arly in their careers are Alfred Lunt, Sydney Greenstreet, John Travolta, Sarah Jessica Parker, Red Skelton, and Cary Grant, to name but a few. And, in the ninety-plus years that have followed its inauguration, The Muny stage has played host to a constellation of visiting performers, such as Bob Hope, Ethel Merman, Cab Calloway, Yul Brynner, Gene Kelly, Richard Harris, Debbie Reynolds, Mitzi Gaynor, Ben Vereen, Richard Roundtree, and Phyllis Diller.

And thus continues the Saint Louis tradition of families coming together from all around the area to enjoy a night of live theatre under the stars.

By the early 1980s, the museum was ready to develop again; to shift from a "behind glass case" environment to the hands-on, learn-by-doing philosophy of a "science center." With the distinctive white, hyperboloid-shaped Planetarium as its new home, the Science Center was an immediate hit. Its success led to another stage of expansion in 1991, when the Science Center increased its size sevenfold. By 2001, the Science Center had become a three-building complex with the addition of the air-supported EXPLORADOME™ adjacent to the Oakland Avenue building, designated to house special traveling exhibitions, more classrooms, and programming space.

Above: The James S. McDonnell Planetarium is one of the most recognized architectural silhouettes in Saint Louis.

Above: The Science Center has more than 700 hands-on exhibits.

Right: The Energizer® Machine is the largest kinetic sculpture machine of its kind in the world. Walking the treadmill is one way to set the machine in motion.

Saint Louis Science Center

The Saint Louis Science Center stands not only as a jewel in the southeast corner of Forest Park, but also as one of the top five science centers in the country, and one of the top six in the world. Innovative exhibits, high-quality educational and public programs, giant-screen films and an entertaining and dynamic staff deliver the Science Center experience, making it a must-visit attraction for both U.S. and international tourists.

Below: The Science Center's main building and James S. McDonnell Planetarium are connected by an enclosed bridge across Interstate 64.

For more information on Saint Louis Science Center
www.slsc.org
5050 Oakland Ave., Saint Louis, MO 63110
Tel. (314) 289 4400

People in the Park

Forest Park is a gathering place for Saint Louisans and our guests, an urban park that is the home for attractions, events and activities that reflect our interests, culture, and history. It is a place in which to experience wonders great and small, natural and man-made—be it an inspiring vista, an endangered species, an Old World masterpiece, real world technology, or a shady glen offering a moment of tranquility. It is a place we share, and a place for which we share responsibility.

The award-winning riffles attract children of all ages to experience the River Returns Project.

For more information on programs contact
Forest Park Forever
www.forestparkforever.org
or visit
http://stlouis.missouri.org/citygov/parks/forest park/

Forest Park provides us with settings to appreciate the world around us, and within ourselves. It is easily accessible, yet free of the constant intrusions of daily life. Here we may walk barefoot in the grass, hear the sweet song of a migratory bird, watch young children catching their first fish or neighbors enjoying a summer's day. We may contemplate a piece of art or architecture, float on the lakes amidst falling autumn leaves, walk silently through a forest on freshly fallen snow, or lie in the fields of wildflowers as spring arrives.

As home to many of our finest cultural institutions, Forest Park is a place to come face-to-face with a baby chimpanzee, take a journey through the Heavens or back in time, hear the stars sing at night, or uncover the secrets of a pharaoh's tomb. It is a place of learning and discovery–of unique experiences that will bring us back again and again.

Left: Every Easter car enthusiasts gather for the annual car show in Forest Park.

Above: Educational programs embrace Forest Park for stimulating and challenging discoveries. Schools and programming utilize the Park as an outdoor classroom.

one enjoys gardening, volunteering
ith the Flora Conservancy is a wonderful
pportunity to plant a variety of flowers in
number of beautiful Park settings—at the
wel Box, in front of The Muny, beside
arkling lakes, and in native prairies and
vannahs. The Flora Conservancy has
eated colorful perennial and annual
ds adjacent to the Jewel Box using plant
aterial donated by local growers and funds
om the Parks Department. Through their
forts, a fountain at the Jewel Box has been
paired, with water once again flowing
om it for the first time in thirty years. The
ounds have become reactivated through
w events, such as the Tulip Festival, which
held every spring by the Flora Conservancy.

Today, the Flora Conservancy is actively
expanding its volunteer association to
include other garden areas within the City
of Saint Louis Parks system including Serra
Park, Lafayette Park, Carondelet Park, and
Soulard Market Park. As a volunteer with the
Flora Conservancy, one may take advantage
of the chance to spend time with fellow
gardeners; to enjoy the outdoors together;
exchange gardening tales, and share valuable
information and experiences. Together, it
is possible to help in the realization of the
restoration plans that will ensure this
historical landmark of grand beauty
continues for all visitors to behold.

Help us decorate the park
before someone else does.

The Flora Conservancy of Forest Park
Because flowers just look better.
To find out how you can volunteer or contribute, call 314-289-5300.

Above and left: The Flora
Conservancy volunteers enhance
park stewardship with an annual
contribution of $500,000 of
in-kind services.

YEARLY FLORAL SHOW SCHEDULE

Show	Season	Flowers / Plants
Poinsettia Show	December / January	Poinsettia
Spring Show	February / March	Azaleas / Spring Bulbs
Lily Show	March / April	Lilies
Hydrangea Show	April / May / June	Hydrangeas
Summer Show	June / July / August / September	Summer Bulbs
Fall Show	October / November	Chrysanthemums / Camellias

The Jewel Box and Gardens

Listed on the National Register of Historic Places, the Saint Louis Floral Conservatory, known as the "Jewel Box," is located in Forest Park on a 17-acre site. The Jewel Box was built by the City of Saint Louis and is operated by the Department of Parks, Recreation and Forestry. The structure was officially dedicated on 14 November 1936 and cost approximately $117,000, with 45% of funding granted from the Works Project Administration (WPA).

Left: The annual Tulip Festival is a popular Spring destination, with over 60,000 tulips in blossom. Commemorative posters are created for each year.

For more information on the Jewel Box, Gardens and Flora Conservancy
http://stlouis.missouri.org/citygov/parks/jewelbox/
www.floraconservancy.org
5600 Clayton Ave., Saint Louis, MO 63110
Tels. (314) 289 5323 and (314) 53FLORA (Volunteer Hotline)

Innovative at its time, glorious in restoration, the Jewel Box is the "crown jewel" of Forest Park.

With its unconventional, cantilevered glass walls rising majestically 50 feet high, the Jewel Box received national acclaim. The *St. Louis Post-Dispatch* called the Art Deco-style structure, "the latest word in display greenhouses." Entrusted for design and oversight of the structure was City engineer William C.E. Becker. His unique design was the result of a year's worth of calculations and testing, with his primary intent to maximize the amount of sunlight into the structure while minimizing maintenance costs resulting from hail damage. The solution he chose was a structure with vertical glass walls, wood and shingle roofs that are horizontal and set back. Its success was demonstrated during a 1938 hailstorm that broke more than 1,000 panes of glass at the nearby municipal greenhouses; the Jewel Box passed the tempest undamaged.

Above and above right: The Jewel Box past and present. Forest Park's private partner, Forest Park Forever, led the restoration of the Jewel Box.

The Jewel Box was an immediate and popular success, attracting more than 400,000 visitors a year in its heyday. The first floral show contained more than 3,00 chrysanthemums in a formal, Chinese-styl display. After being open for only three months, electric lighting was added to allow visitors more time to see the shows.

The Flora Conservancy

The outdoor gardens at the Jewel Box are ongoing and continue to be developed through volunteer efforts by the Flora Conservancy, a unique not-for-profit organization established in 1999 in partnership with the Saint Louis Department of Parks, Recreation and Forestry. The Flora Conservancy was originally created to assist in the implementation of the Forest Park Master Plan. Flora volunteers work a year-round, flexible schedule, providing horticultural services in design, enhancement, and maintenance of the Park's gardens, savannahs, and prairies. On-site training of volunteers is provided by the Saint Louis Master Gardeners and by the City Horticulture staff. Volunteers are educated in everything from soil structure and amending, plant production and identification, and garden installation and design.

Above: The Treehugger sculpture was constructed as an environmentally sensitive public art installation.

Pansies and Tulips make for the rotating annual gardens on the grounds of the Jewel Box.

In all that it does, the Science Center remains focused on its central mission—to stimulate an interest in, and understanding of, science and technology throughout the community. The Academy forefathers wanted to open up the world to Saint Louisans through their collections. Almost 150 years later, it is the marvels and wonders of twenty-first-century science that attract and inspire the millions of visitors that come to the Saint Louis Science Center each year.

Right: The catenary arch activity remains a favorite among Science Center visitors.

Left: The Zeiss Universarium Mark IX projector displays more than 9,000 stars on an 80-foot dome.

Right: No visit to the Science Center is complete without a stop at the famous animatronic T-Rex.

Its roots date back to 1856 and to the Academy of Science of Saint Louis. As part of the city's flourishing mercantilism of the time, a group of wealthy and well-traveled businessmen created the Academy and a museum in which to display their considerable collections of fauna, cultural artifacts, and scientific items. By 1959, the Academy had evolved—with the help of additional collections and an educational staff—into the Museum of Science and Natural History, and moved to Clayton's Oak Knoll Park. For the next twenty-five years, the museum was an integral part of school field trips for youngsters of the area.

Above: Overnight Camp-Ins are a popular Science Center program. They include an OMNIMAX® film or a Space Show, themed activities, and "camping" in the Science Center.

As a center of recreational activity, Forest Park teems with athletes and sports enthusiasts at all levels, ages, and skills. Its paths, field, courses, and courts allow those involved in each activity the freedom to enjoy the park without limiting the enjoyment of others.

As a focal point for special events, Forest Park gives us reasons to celebrate our heritage, our hopes, and our happiness. Our gatherings here help define our community and demonstrate the warmth, wonder, and friendships that we share.

Nowhere else can we share the variety and totality of experiences that Forest Park provides. The strength of the park flows from that sharing, from our willingness and ability to protect the park for all of us in all of our uses. Forest Park is more than a symbol of the beauty and tradition of Saint Louis; it is a place where we define our community and celebrate our pluralism every day.

Saint Louis 2004 celebrated the 200th anniversary of Lewis and Clark's Corps of Discovery expedition to the West, exploring the Louisiana Purchase and the 100th anniversary of the 1904 World's Fair in Forest Park.

Left: The Balloon Glow and the Great Forest Park Balloon Race attracts over 100,000 citizens and over 70 hot air balloons to race across the region.